GEORGE GERSHWIN®

olo

"I GOT RHYTHM"
VARIATIONS

Edited and Transcribed by Dr. Alicia Zizzo
(Based on a Work by George Gershwin and Ira Gershwin)

To
My Brother Ira

Project Manager: Tony Esposito
Music Editor: Ethan Neuburg
Book Art Layout: Lisa Greene Mane

Preface

The genesis of the song "I Got Rhythm" began with *Treasure Girl* (1928) as a slow number and ultimately found its way into *Girl Crazy* (1930) as the song we know today.

George Gershwin was rich and successful and two years away from his goal of finding a composition teacher who would help him expand his compositional skills. Over a period of time, he had been turned down by Nadia Boulanger, Maurice Ravel, and Alexander Glazunov, respectively. According to Edward Jablonski in his book *George Gershwin: A Biography* (Doubleday 1987), Gershwin finally connected with Josef Schillinger in 1932 and studied with him until 1936. In Mr. Jablonski's words: "In short, the [Schillinger] system was strong on technique, weak on originality (or that elusive thing, 'inspiration'; if the gift is missing, not all the mathematics in the world is a substitute)."

George Gershwin, however, lacked neither inspiration nor originality, but Schillinger's methodology of creating a mathematical grid as the basis of composition seemed to satisfy Gershwin's desire to formalize his creative genius within a structured framework. He was clearly preparing himself for a future in serious modern composition. "Cuban Overture," "I Got Rhythm Variations," "Second Rhapsody," *Porgy and Bess,* and his final shows, including the movie score for *Shall We Dance,* were all composed during this period.

Sometime in 1933, Gershwin had begun clearing his schedule in anticipation of his forthcoming opera *Porgy and Bess*. He concurrently signed a contract for a weekly radio broadcast he would host, and also arranged for a cross-country concert tour in celebration of the tenth anniversary of his "Rhapsody in Blue." His notion of creating for himself a window of time seems remarkable, but intense schedules were nothing new for Gershwin and this spate of activity was no exception, save a brief respite in Palm Beach, Florida. There he dashed off his "I Got Rhythm Variations" (almost as an afterthought). Perhaps he had realized there was a dearth of his own classical material for his concert tour. How fortuitous for us!

In one of his radio broadcasts, on February 19, 1934, Gershwin unassumingly describes his marvelous new piece. He relates to his radio audience that the work begins quietly, with the orchestra artlessly introducing the four-note theme. When the piano finally enters, it, too, articulates the theme simply. He goes on to say that in the first variation, the piano plays a complicated rhythmic pattern while the orchestra plays the theme. This variation is perky and quirky. Next comes "Valse Triste" (Gershwin's title in his manuscript). It moves along at a waltz tempo, but it is devoid of the romantic elements found in most waltzes and is rather dissonant as the violins squeal with glissandos, forging a certain ersatz pathos. The third variation imitates Chinese flutes played out of tune "as they always are" according to George. In describing his fourth variation, Gershwin does not refer to it during the radio broadcast as a jazz variation. He tells us that the melody is played upside down by the left hand while the right hand plays it straight "on the theory: never let one hand know what the other is doing." The finale follows. It is complicated and energetic, and interestingly, within its closing moments one hears for the first time a new voice inhabiting the end of the piece. It appears twice, gently escorting the departing tune in its final iterations. This secondary theme provides a quasi-poignant goodbye to the listener before it runs away from us with a wink and a bang!

The task of transcribing a piece as complex as "I Got Rhythm Variations" was enormous. I felt obliged to maintain the integrity of the interrelated group of variations with their individual ideas as they formed an integrated whole. In order to reduce successfully the thousands of notes an entire orchestra plays in this work to two hands, I had to develop a deep understanding of the intricate and elegant weaving of Gershwin's harmonies as he continually reworked four little notes. I determined that I would preserve as many chordal, verbal, and dynamic directives as ten fingers would allow. To succeed at this, I turned to three sources: "I Got Rhythm Variations" for two pianos, four hands, arranged in 1935 by Gregory Stone, and published in *The Complete Gershwin® Keyboard Works* (Warner Bros. Publications), and of critical importance, Gershwin's two manuscripts in his own hand, dated January 6, 1934. The first is a piano sketch of the entire piece. It contains valuable information. The second is the full orchestration of the work. My extensive study of these two manuscripts yielded harmonies and rhythmic motifs that lent themselves extremely well to the fulfillment of a richly textured piano solo transcription, in which certain tempos and dynamics had to be dealt with given the confines of the solo piano.

Acknowledgments

With many thanks to:

Leopold Godowsky III for his high musical ideals, which served as an inspiration to me. I am in his debt.

The Gershwin Estate and especially Marc George Gershwin.

Edward Jablonski, my mentor and dear friend, without whom I could not have moved forward.

Avraham Sternklar, master pianist and composer, whose scholarship, comradeship, and encouragement were always with me.

Ethan Neuburg for his professionalism and dignity throughout this project.

Joseph Bartolozzi, Finale copyist for my original manuscripts.

"I GOT RHYTHM" VARIATIONS

for Piano Solo

Based on a work by
GEORGE GERSHWIN and IRA GERSHWIN
Transcribed and Edited by ALICIA ZIZZO

Moderato ♩ = 80 *(not strictly in tempo)*

*sostenuto Ped.

*Catch only the chord with sost. pedal.

AFM01011

*Cross over is optional.
**Bring out upper note.

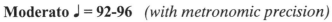

Moderato ♩ = 92-96 *(with metronomic precision)*

*Tenuto marks are editor's suggestion.

*Easier: Omit low B♭.
**Easier: Play chords as eighth notes, eliminating sixteenth notes.

*Woodwinds, bells (reference only).
**Slurs not in original score.

*Vivace in 2 piano edition, Allegro in original score.
**♩= 108 in original score, ♩ = 120 in 2 piano edition.
***Gliss. in original score performed by violins 8va and 15ma.

*Accel. is editor's suggestion.

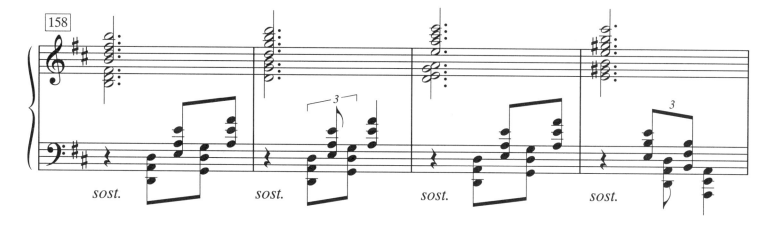

*Performance note: Pedal triplets (every other measure).
****Resoluto** in 2 piano edition.

AFM01011

14

*Easier: omit bottom note of chords.
**Rit. not in original score.

mf in manuscript.

**Performance note: Bring out theme in l.h.

*Suggested tempo.
**Slurs not in original manuscript.
***l.h. crescendos/decrescendos optional (orchestral dynamics).
****Easier: Omit middle note.

*Optional grace notes.
**Optional *rit.*

Allegro assai ♩ = 120

Allegretto ♩ = 104

Flutes, oboes

molto dim.

**rit.

sost.

* ♩ = **136** in original score.
**Optional *rit.* (Original score).
***Optional fermata (not in original score).
****Reference only.

*See Appendix.
**Editor's note: This section is improvised with a "walking" bass.

mf in original manuscript.

*See Appendix.
**Editor's suggestion.
***Cresc. not in original manuscript.

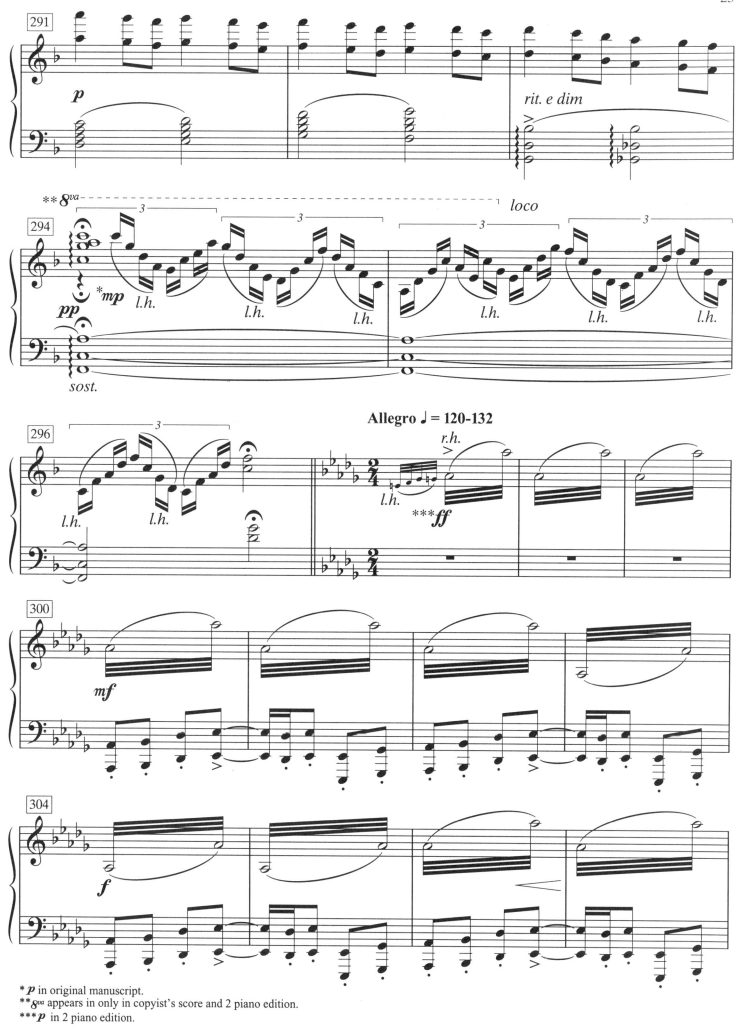

* *p* in original manuscript.
** *8va* appears in only in copyist's score and 2 piano edition.
*** *p* in 2 piano edition.

*See Appendix.

*Editor's suggestion.

**Suggested tempo.

***Accents in original piano sketch only. In both the 2 piano
published edition and full orchestration, accents are omitted.

****Easier: reduce l.h. chords to 3 notes each or octaves only.

N.B.: To accomodate the solo pianist, arrangement includes some shift in register.

*See Appendix.
**Easier: Play as rolled half note.

Allegro

*Opt.: Bottom notes of chords can be tied for easier performance.
**Slurs and accents are editorial suggestions.
***See Appendix.

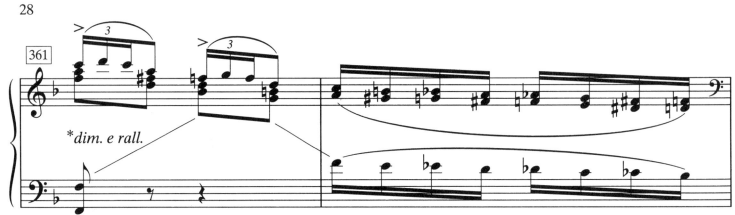

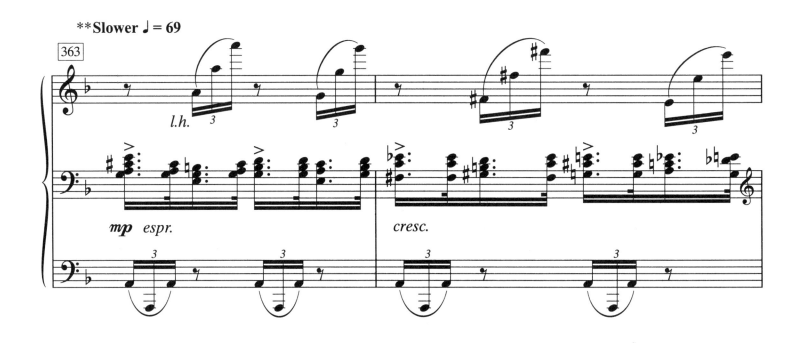

* Editor's suggestion.
** Tempo is editor's suggestion. Actual tempo in score is still **Allegro**.

*See Appendix.

30

*Eighth notes in l.h. are editor's suggestion. Actual score uses quarter notes (displayed here in cue size).
**See Appendix.

Appendix

Editor's suggestions, annotations, and comments are based on "I Got Rhythm Variations" for two pianos, four hands, (2 Piano), George Gershwin's original score (ms) and the original piano sketch (ps) housed at the Library of Congress.

Bars 1–6, 11–14: Hairpin cresc. not found in either orch. score or piano sketch, but appears in two-piano edition.

Bar 1: In GG ms: *mp*; Bar 7: *p*; Bar 9: $\quad$ = 100

Bar 21: *mp*; Bars 21–26: In ms, first violins are *f*, and orch. is *p*.
Ed. sugg: Play bars 19–26 *una corda* as *pp*.

Bars 32–39: No ⟨ ⟩ indicated in ms.

Bars 70–95: Note displaced accent on second sixteenth note of the second beat. Bar 70: *mf* in ms.

Bar 73: *molto rall.* is editor's suggestion.

Bar 79: $\quad$ = 92 in ms. GG plays it at 96 in 1934 radio broadcast.

Bars 100–101 and 106–107: Ossia measures for reference only.

Bar 124: *Sordini* (muted) indicated in ms.

Bar 127: **Allegro**, $\quad$ = 132 in GG ms.

Bar 131: In orch. ms $\quad$ = 108, but a slower tempo is suggested for solo piano.
Easier to play: Bars 131–138: Omit *l.h.* quarter notes in treble clef and play *una corda* using the sustain pedal instead of the sost. ped.

Bars 157–164: Ed. suggestion: Distinguish between triplets and eighth-note groups in bass clef by using ped. only on triplets.

Bar 174: **Allegretto giocoso** is $\quad$ = 108 in ms, but $\quad$ = 92 is suggested for this variation for solo piano.

Bars 201–206: Easier: Omit grace notes on upper octaves.

Bar 217: Catch bass clef chord with sost. pedal, and pick up second sixteenth note in middle treble clef with *l.h.*

Bar 253: Alternate suggestion: Break the tied B♭ *l.h.* note (first beat) and replace with the following:

Bars 262–281: In the original orchestra manuscript, there is no piano part. The walking bass provided here appears in the original piano sketch in Gershwin's own hand. It provides a steady 4/4 beat that confirms its jazzy texture. It is also not present in the two-piano arrangement.

Bars 268–271: Chords should be played unbroken, if possible, to avoid losing jazz momentum.

Bars 268–270: Easier: Play only top notes of sixteenth octaves.

Bars 272–275: *Espressivo* does not appear in either ms or ps. This passage is a flute solo and can be played *una corda*. Staccatos are in the GG ms.

Bars 283–284 and 287–288: Ed. suggestion: For a different texture, play the runs on the fourth beats of 283/287 and the first beats of 284/288 one octave lower.

Bars 297–327: Ed. suggestion: Because the orchestral build-up in this **Allegro** section is gradual and tense, one might wish to take some liberties with the score. The piano introduces the section (bars 297–300). The orchestra then enters with cellos, basses, and bassoons. The steady textured orchestral build-up creates a challenge for piano solo. One option is to shift some registers without losing momentum. Example: Bars 297–307: Both hands remain unchanged. Bars 308–309, 312–313, and 316–317: Right hand drops one octave lower and left hand remains unchanged. In bars 320–325, the right hand plays *loco* (no 8va) and the left hand plays one octave higher, thus bringing the registers closer. Listen to the orchestrated piece before reaching your own individual conclusion.

Bar 328: No metronome markings appear in any score, but a slower tempo than the preceding sections works well for solo piano.

Bar 340: Easier: Both hands omit chords in upper register and repeat the triplets on the second half of the first beat. Omit *rit*.

Bar 342: Easier: *l.h.* plays first beat as a rolled half-note chord; *r.h.* repeats chord (in the same register as beat 1). Omit upper system *l.h.*

Bar 340

Bar 342

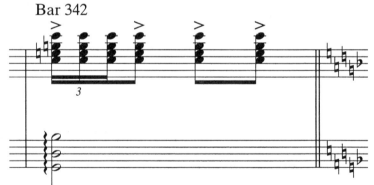

Bars 355–357: Ed. suggestion: To create textural space, omit *l.h.* beginning with the second half of the first beat. Do not tie bottom chord notes, and use both hands to play the theme. Bass re-enters in bar 359.

Bar 355

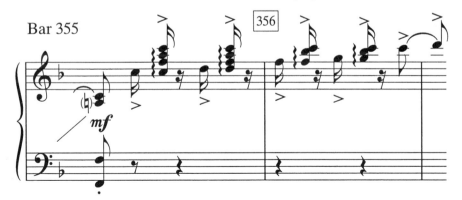

Bass re-enters:

Bar 363: No change of tempo is indicated in ms. However, crossing hands need time, and a slower tempo better articulates the beauty of the section for solo piano.

Bars 365–366: Ed. suggestion: Incorporate first notes of upper staff triplets into the *r.h.*

Bars 374 and 376: Ed. suggestion: In orch. ms, trills are supported by strings. The following works well on the piano:

Bars 379–381: In the ms, violins play the theme while the piano accompanies. Second violins, violas, winds, and horns support with eighth notes critical to the momentum.

Bar 382: *Finale* (**Maestoso moderato**) Optional: An alternate ending is included here to accommodate the reoccurrence of the finale's secondary theme, which appears in this piece for the first time. In the orchestral version, this theme repeats once, underlying the ascending triplets in bars 386–388. Additionally, the final statement of the theme is large and exciting in the orchestral arrangement and may be satisfied as a piano solo by the ascending triplets of the final theme to its conclusion, as found in the alternate ending.

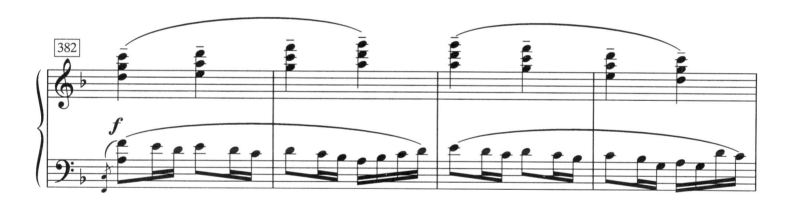

Dr. Alicia Zizzo
Pianist and Musicologist

Biographical Sketch

As one of America's most important classical musicians, Dr. Alicia Zizzo's pianistic artistry has taken her to stages in London (the Barbican Center), Amsterdam (the Concertgebouw), Vienna (the Musikverein), Budapest (the Vigado, with the Budapest Symphony), Warsaw (The Ostrovsky Palace for the Chopin Society), New York (Avery Fisher Hall and Carnegie Hall) as well as other European venues and throughout the U.S. She has also been invited to participate in symposiums, conferences, and lectures/recitals at major American universities. She is a Steinway Artist (www.steinway.com).

Dr. Zizzo's musicological scholarship has been focused primarily on the research and restoration of the classical piano literature of George Gershwin. Specifically, Alicia Zizzo's goal has been to enhance his remarkably small classical piano solo repertoire. Working with the Library of Congress, Warner Bros. Publications, the Gershwin estate and leading Gershwin scholar Edward Jablonski, she has researched, studied, and reconstructed the composer's lost or forgotten classical solo piano manuscripts notated in his own hand. She approaches Gershwin's manuscripts not with the objective of making yet another arrangement of his melodies as so many musicians have already done, but rather to literally reconstruct from fragments, sketches, and partially completed scores Gershwin's own long neglected material.

Warner Bros. Publications, which administers all copyrights to Gershwin's material, has made Dr. Zizzo's reconstructions of *Lullaby, Blue Monday, The Complete Seven Preludes,* the *Annotated Rhapsody in Blue, The I Got Rhythm Variations* for piano solo, and other unpublished manuscripts for solo piano the first new authentic editions of Gershwin classical material to be published in more than half a century. Warner Bros. is online at www.warnerbrospublications.com.

Her work has been hailed in dozens of magazines and newspapers on four continents, ranging from *The New York Times, Washington Post,* and *Boston Globe* to Canada's *Toronto Star* to Tokyo's *Asahi Shimbun* to Taiwan's *China Post* to London's *Gramophone* and *Classic FM Magazine* to the Netherlands' *NRC Handelsblad* to Bogota's *El Espectador.* Her groundbreaking musicological analysis of the original manuscripts of *Rhapsody in Blue* was published internationally in *Clavier* magazine. She has also written about Gershwin's "lost" preludes for this magazine and others, including *Piano & Keyboard* and *Piano Today.*

Dr. Zizzo has appeared on NBC's "Today Show"; ABC's evening news; the BBC World Service; WLIW TV (PBS New York); BBC Radio Four; CNN; the Voice of America; National Public Radio in Washington, Boston, and New York; KKGO-San Francisco; WGBH-Boston; Canada's CBC; and Radio France (both the France Musique and Musique Lundi programs). She also appeared and performed in a major National Public Radio documentary celebrating Gershwin's 100th birthday. She has also participated in film documentaries about Gershwin for the noted French filmmaker Alain Resnais, as well as for the BBC Wales, the latter of which was filmed at the Library of Congress.

Dr. Zizzo's landmark CDs *Gershwin Rediscovered* (Carlton Classics 30366-00052) and *Gershwin Rediscovered,* Volume II (Carlton Classics 30366-00312) featured her superbly idiomatic performances of these lost manuscripts, including the completely restored *Rhapsody in Blue* (both the solo piano and orchestral versions), Concerto in F, *Seven Preludes, Blue Monday, Lullaby,* and a series of lovely miniatures, including *Sleepless Night.* These performances added to the recorded repertoire her major discoveries on Gershwin's music and will be reissued in 2003.

Dr. Zizzo has also recorded these discoveries and reconstructions for MSR Piano Disc.

Her latest CD is *Rhythm & Hues,* which features the piano suite from *Shall We Dance, The I Got Rhythm Variations* for piano solo, and other unpublished manuscripts for solo piano, as well as the *The Complete Seven Preludes* counterpointed with selected Chopin preludes. *Piano Dreams* has also recently been issued on the Musicians Showcase Recordings label (MS1053) and is being used in the soundtrack of a new film being produced in Canada.

Classic CD called the Carlton Classics CDs "undoubtedly fascinating releases" and also said "anyone listening to Zizzo's performance of *Rhapsody in Blue,* based directly on the composer's manuscript, is bound to notice some striking differences. . . . The inclusion of extra transitional material . . . certainly serves to strengthen the structural coherence of the whole work."

London's *Classic FM* magazine has written: "There's plenty of excitement . . . in *Gershwin Rediscovered* . . . scintillatingly played by Zizzo from the manuscript Gershwin used in his own performances. The piece emerges as much wittier and more intricate than the published version we usually hear." *Gramophone* magazine has said: "Future Gershwin pianists will need to come to terms with Zizzo's discoveries . . . really charming discoveries."

In a four-day celebration of the Gershwin Centennial in 1998, an impressive roster of the most renowned Gershwin scholars and musicians were invited to make presentations at the Coolidge Auditorium of the Library of Congress in Washington, D.C. Among them were Michael Feinstein, Michael Tilson Thomas, Anne Wiggins Brown (the original "Bess" in *Porgy and Bess*) and Edward Jablonski. Alicia Zizzo was honored to be the only concert pianist invited to present a full recital and lecture at this historic event. She performed her Gershwin/Zizzo publications and received the highest laudatory praise.

Along with honorees George Bush and Billy Joel, Alicia Zizzo was awarded an honorary doctorate degree by Hofstra University in recognition of her important contributions to American music.

Her Web page is at www.jamesarts.com/zizzo.gershwin.htm. Her *Rhapsody* newsletter is online at www.jamesarts.com/releases/jan03/AZ_nws_010503.htm. You can read several of her important articles about Gershwin's music online at www.jamesarts.com/releases/march03/AZ_030303.htm, www.jamesarts.com/releases/nov02/AZ_112602.htm, www.jamesarts.com/AZRHAPNOTE.htm, and www.jamesarts.com/AZCLAVPREL.htm.

She can also be contacted through Jeffrey James Arts Consulting, 316 Pacific St., Massapequa Park, NY 11762, 516-797-9166 (phone and fax) or at jamesarts@worldnet.att.net.